TRUE DECEIT
FALSE LOVE

*Survivor's Acrostic Poetry Workbook
on Domestic Violence, Narcissistic
Abuse & Parental Alienation*

DR. MARNI HILL FODERARO

BALBOA.PRESS
A DIVISION OF HAY HOUSE

Balboa Press books may be ordered through booksellers or by contacting:

Balboa Press
A Division of Hay House
1663 Liberty Drive
Bloomington, IN 47403
www.balboapress.com
844-682-1282

Print information available on the last page.

ISBN: 978-1-9822-7921-9 (sc)
ISBN: 978-1-9822-7922-6 (e)

Library of Congress Control Number: 2022901527

Balboa Press rev. date: 01/24/2022

DISCLAIMER

The terms, phrases and poems provided in this book and in the ***TRUE DECEIT FALSE LOVE*** series of books are on an "as is" basis and intended for informational, educational and entertainment purposes only and should not be understood to constitute a medical, psychological or psychiatric diagnosis, healthcare recommendation or legal advice. The author's intent through these original acrostic poems is to build awareness and provide linguistic examples, definitions, descriptions and/or responses to understand and heal from the trauma of experiencing Domestic Violence, Narcissistic Abuse and/or Parental Alienation. The author and publisher make no representations or warranties of any kind with respect to the contents of this book and assume no responsibility for errors, inaccuracies, omissions or any other inconsistencies herein. Reading these terms, phrases and acrostic poems are at your own risk and you agree to take full responsibility for any resulting consequences. The information in this book is not a substitution for direct expert assistance and may be triggering. Please seek legal advice or professional help from a medical, psychological, psychiatrist or healthcare specialist if necessary. The author did not develop any of these terms and phrases, as they were coined by countless others, and is not an expert or licensed provider on Domestic Violence, Narcissistic Abuse and/or Parental Alienation, is not responsible for any resulting consequences, and the use of this book implies your acceptance of this disclaimer. The opinions, roles and responses expressed in the poems are general and should not be confused with the opinions of the author. Certain agencies, businesses and professionals are mentioned for reference purposes only, however characters, roles, genders, events and incidents are the products of the author's imagination. Any resemblance to actual persons, living or dead, male or female, young or old or actual events is purely coincidental.

ENDORSEMENTS

*   *   *

"Marni Hill Foderaro's acrostic poems in ***TRUE DECEIT FALSE LOVE*** reveal the cruelty of Narcissistic Abuse. She understands the twisted reality, the devastation in recognizing it and the loss associated with escape. Readers who have walked this path—and particularly those whose children have been alienated by an ex-spouse—will feel understood, thus less alone. Even those well-versed in the Narcissistic Abuse vernacular will find some new terminology to label their experiences. The format allows for short reading sessions, so as not to overwhelm the more sensitive Trauma Survivor, yet prompts deeper contemplation. Marni's perspectives cut straight to the heart … and pave the way to healing."

~ **Sheri McGregor,** M.A., Life Coach, RejectedParents.NET Founder/ Blogger and Author of the books *"Beyond Done: More Answers and Advice for Parents of Estranged Adult Children"* (2021) and *"Done With The Crying: Help and Healing for Mothers of Estranged Adult Children"* (2016)

*   *   *

"Dr. Marni Hill Foderaro brilliantly provides much needed hope and validation when speaking to your heart and explaining to the reader that there is a way through this dark and tangled mess. This inspirational series, *TRUE DECEIT FALSE LOVE*, with her insightful books of terms, phrases and acrostic poetry, along with a companion workbook for survivors, is a must-read resource manual for anyone who finds themselves embarking on the challenging journey through Narcissistic Abuse and Parental Alienation. As she quite rightly says, words have a way of hurting you, but words also have a way of healing. Marni's creative use of words will guide you in transcending pain and empowering you on your healing journey."

~**Anoushka Marcin,** Psychologist Practitioner, Top UK Narcissistic and Trauma Abuse Expert, Owner of @balance.psychologies, Well-Being Blogger and Podcaster

* * *

"When we're able to apply the proper language to what we're mentally and emotionally experiencing, we're able to create personal clarity, it helps others to understand what we're currently experiencing and allows us to open the door to finding solutions and to eventually work to heal from the abuse that we have endured. Dr. Marni Hill Foderaro's ingenious work focusing on Domestic Violence, Narcissistic Abuse and Parental Alienation allows the reader to understand, discover and fully realize what they have been experiencing. Often the victims blame themselves for what is taking place and are unable to see the full picture. Dr. Marni, through her *TRUE DECEIT FALSE LOVE* series, offers terms and phrases, poetry and a workbook to help victims to be able to stop blaming themselves, to see the participants clearly and begin to safeguard their inner person. When we understand the truth of what we're experiencing, we're able to find solution, work to end the abuse and stop the cycle. We then begin the healing phase of our personal journey and stop engaging with what no longer serves our highest good."

~**Ashley Berges,** Nationally Syndicated Radio Talk Show Host of "Live Your True Life Perspectives," International Award-winning podcast, the Live Your True Life Coach and Author of *"The 10 Day Challenge to Live Your True Life"*

* * *

"It becomes clear, once you read the writings of Dr. Marni Hill Foderaro, your heart and mind will unlock from your abuser and you can begin a healing journey of recovery from Narcissistic Abuse, Toxic Relationships, Parental Alienation and Childhood Trauma, which are exposed for what they are: a painful pandemic on the Human Family. The *TRUE DECEIT FALSE LOVE* series of books is a resourceful emotional abuse recovery and reference tool full of time-released treasures and solid golden nuggets."

~Paxton, NarcAbuse TV Host

* * *

"Dr. Marni Hill Foderaro empowers readers with knowledge and unconditional love on their healing journey from Narcissistic Abuse. The *TRUE DECEIT FALSE LOVE* series of books provides deep insight, validation, education and support to those who are healing from emotional abuse and sabotage on their life journey. This resourceful series of books offers much hope to those who are working to recover the truth of themselves before abuse and alienation. Dr. Marni Hill Foderaro is helping to transform trauma and bring more light to this world, and I enthusiastically recommend her books."

~Tricia Barker, Near Death Experiencer, YouTuber, Intuitive, Medium, Professor, *Author of "Angels in the OR: What Dying Taught Me About Healing, Survival and Transformation"* and *"Loving Narcissus & Sometimes God: Poems"*

* * *

"*TRUE DECEIT FALSE LOVE* exposes the truth of narcissists and betrayal. An unfortunate circumstance for anyone to go through, but something that we can all learn and grow from. Let Dr. Marni Hill Foderaro's thought-provoking writing validate your experiences and guide you to finding your survivor's voice."

~Narc Survivor, Life Coach & CEO of Narc Survivor Ltd.

Realizing that you've experienced Family Abuse, expressing your ordeal and healing from Domestic Trauma can be challenging. To help you on your healing journey, please refer to the words in the first (blue) volume of this series:

TRUE DECEIT FALSE LOVE: 15,555 Terms & Phrases on Domestic Violence, Narcissistic Abuse & Parental Alienation

In the second (green) volume of the series, these terms & phrases were used to inspire alphabetical acrostic poems. There are 13 poems for each of the 26 letters of the alphabet, resulting in 338 acrostic poems.

TRUE DECEIT FALSE LOVE: Alphabetical Acrostic Anthems on Domestic Violence, Narcissistic Abuse & Parental Alienation

This corresponding third (red) volume of the series is a Survivor's Acrostic Poetry Workbook, where the reader is able to personally create, write and author his or her own acrostic poems. For each letter of the alphabet there are suggested terms & phrases, 1 completed poem for an example, 2 poem recommendations and 3 lined pages for words/poems of your own choosing. This results in 6 poems for each of the 26 letters of the alphabet, so there will be 156 poems when the workbook is completed.

TRUE DECEIT FALSE LOVE: Survivor's Acrostic Poetry Workbook on Domestic Violence, Narcissistic Abuse & Parental Alienation

When you finally realize that you've been a victim of Family Violence at the hands of a malevolent, calculating abuser, someone you cared for and loved unconditionally, finding the words to understand the methodical gaslighting and deliberate smearing you've endured can be exceptionally challenging.

**Language has the power to hurt,
but language also has the power to heal.**

Reading, writing and creating your own acrostic poems can be extremely therapeutic on your healing journey from Family Abuse and Domestic Trauma. In time, the abuser's mask slips and with your own research, investigation and creative outlet (like reading and writing acrostic poetry) you will come to understand the truth, find your survivor's voice and reclaim your life.

**Will there be a fourth volume in the *TRUE
DECEIT FALSE LOVE* series?**

**How will these terms & phrases be used?
Will the next book cover be yellow?**

**Realizing you've experienced Family Abuse, expressing your ordeal
and healing from the Domestic Trauma you have endured can
be challenging. The terms, phrases and acrostic poems in *TRUE
DECEIT FALSE LOVE* will help you on your healing journey.**

When you finally realize that you've been a victim of Family Violence at the hands of a malevolent, calculating abuser, someone you cared for and loved unconditionally, finding the words to understand the methodical gaslighting, deliberate smearing and significant losses you've endured and then to be able to understand, express and heal from your trauma can be especially challenging. Language has the power to hurt, but language also has the power to heal. The acrostic poems in Books 2 and 3 of the ***TRUE DECEIT FALSE LOVE*** series of books provide information on and an emotional, experiential response to many terms & phrases on Domestic Violence, Narcissistic Abuse & Parental Alienation, as well as Intergenerational Family Trauma. Reading and creating these acrostic poems may result in much-needed validation as you reflect on what you've been through while you connect the dots to your own experiences. Writing can help make sense of your emotions and experiences and can be extremely therapeutic on your healing journey. In time, the abuser's mask slips, and with your own research and creative outlet, you will come to understand the truth, find your survivor's voice, reclaim your authenticity and live a blessed and happy life filled with abundance, gratitude and love.

DEDICATION

This book is dedicated to the victims and survivors of Domestic Violence, Narcissistic Abuse and/or Parental Alienation, as well as Intergenerational Family Trauma. Bringing forth awareness is especially needed for the innocent young and adult children that are strategically used as destructive weapons to unjustly reject their targeted, loving parent and their entire side of that family. These abused children are unknowingly aligned with, dependent on and trauma-bonded with the malevolent, mentally unstable manipulator. My heart goes out to all the men, women and children that have experienced this traumatic Intergenerational Family Trauma and Marital Partner Terrorism and I sincerely believe in my heart that truth, love and goodness will eventually prevail.

To my beautiful children from their loving mom:

"If you're feeling frightened about what comes next, don't be. Embrace the uncertainty. Allow it to lead you places. Be brave as it challenges you to exercise both your heart and your mind as you create your own path towards happiness, don't wast time with regret. Spin wildly into your next action.

Enjoy the present, each moment, as it comes; because you'll never get another one quite like it, and if you should ever look up and find yourself lost, simply take a breath and start over. Retrace your steps and go back to the purest place in your heart...where your hope lives. You'll find your way again.

Because sometimes you have something you need to say, but you can't because the words won't come out, or you get scared, or you feel stupid. But if you could write a song and sing it, then you could say what you needed to say, and it would be beautiful, and people would listen, and you wouldn't make a complete idiot out of yourself. But all of us can't be song writers, so some of us will never get the chance to say what we're thinking, or what we want other people to know that we're thinking, so we'll never get the chance to make things right again, ever."

~Rory, Gilmore Girls

PREFACE

A Heartfelt Note From The Author

When you realize that you have been the target of Domestic Violence, Narcissistic Abuse and/or Parental Alienation at the hands of someone you cared for and trusted with unconditional love, in some cases unknowingly enduring this Intimate Partner Terrorism and Intergenerational Family Abuse for decades, your entire world is turned upside down.

After the initial shock of realizing that you ignored years of glaring Red Flags as you were significantly betrayed and deceitfully manipulated, you muster up the courage to escape in the hopes that you can reclaim your life before it's too late. You acknowledge that there are huge repercussions to leaving your abuser. Life as you knew it will never be the same. Your mind races as you now have to consider your basic safety and survival needs of food, shelter, money, transportation and employment. There are family ties for most, and we must contemplate the consequences and impact of our choices on others, especially our immediate family. Some of us are forced to stay because we lack the inner strength or resources to go, are afraid of or don't think we are capable of making such a drastic change or we have young children with our abuser and instinctively must look out for our children's safety and wellbeing. Other victims take time to carefully get their affairs and assets in order so that they have a better chance at a more comfortable exit. Many of us just follow our gut instincts using our best judgment and remove ourselves from the toxic environment at our earliest chance, leaving without a well-thought-out plan.

Abusers and Alienators are predators and they don't usually let their prey go easily or without a fight. Most of these destructive individuals have traits of Mental Illness and if they would ever seek professional help or diagnosis for their condition, a medical, psychological or psychiatric practitioner might label them as a Cluster B, Covert Malignant Narcissist, Psychopath and/or Sociopath. No two abusers are alike as each person's behavior and personality falls on a spectrum of severity. Many of these abusers want to discredit and destroy their targets, especially when the truth of the abuser's behaviors may be exposed. However, they all seem to feel they are above the law and that society's rules don't apply to them; that's why they are so cutthroat and dishonest. They believe in their false perceived power of superiority and somehow they all follow the same general playbook, so their extremely malevolent behaviors are often textbook predictable.

Significant harm is caused to innocent victims as these scheming abusers are known to methodically gaslight their targets for years. These abusers mirror your positive traits and values because they are like empty vessels who lack empathy and morals, yet strive to fit into the mainstream to carry out their dirty and devious deeds. In the beginning of the relationship they state they like and care about all of the same things that you do. You are put on a pedestal as the Love Bombing and Future Faking sucks you into the illusion that you have finally met your soulmate. You pinch yourself because the relationship seems too good to be true. You may believe your life is now like a fairytale as you eventually settle comfortably into living the coveted "American Dream."

Over time, however, you begin to feel confused and experience bouts of Cognitive Dissonance as the abuser acts one way around others, flaunting their created public persona to maintain their false image, and another way with you behind closed doors. You may begin to doubt yourself, your discernment or your abilities. Your physical health suffers and you may develop autoimmune disorders because slowly, without you knowing it, your body and mind have been in "fight or flight" survival mode. Eventually your identity and perspectives are so fundamentally distorted due to the inflicted trauma that you lose your previously solid confidence and find yourself dependent on your abuser as he/she now has the authority over the purse strings and everything in your environment, including who you can see, what you can do and where and when you can go. Your abuser's controlling actions are different than his/her words. You are trapped and stifled with little or no freedom, but you accept your circumstances because these constraints are done under the cloak of care and concern for your wellbeing. Besides, you are busy focusing on your job, home and family, honoring the vows you made under God and have invested so much time and commitment to this relationship that you plug along thinking and trusting things will get better as you hope for the best.

These calculating perpetrators begin to accuse you and others of their own wrongdoings and unethical or illegal activities. Behind your back, they smear your name to everyone and anyone with outlandish lies and believable half-truths. They gain support and sympathy by blame shifting and playing the victim. They brainwash your children, family, friends, neighbors, coworkers and countless others in cult-like fashion to believe that you are a bad or sick person who should be avoided and feared. They accuse their targets of cheating, stealing and lying, when the truth is that they are the ones cheating, stealing and lying. What these ruthless abusers do is called Projection and it is done with such careful planning and malevolent intent, setting the stage for when the relationship will eventually dissolve. In addition to their numerous extramarital escapades, these secret agents keep in contact with old flames and are always on the prowl to line up replacement relationships from their Harem Closet in the event they choose to discard you as their main source of supply, or worse yet for the abuser, you become wise to their games and choose to leave them.

It's usually not until after you separate from the abuser that you realize you are left with no support system or money; your lifelong friends and long-term neighbors become Flying Monkeys who do the bidding for the abuser and give you the cold shoulder, wanting nothing to do with you anymore. It's shocking because you thought that these close relationships were strong and you took for granted that they would always be there for you. In stealth fashion, the abusers utilize the Divide and Conquer method and focus their Campaign of Denigration on those closest to us, so even your relationships with family members surprisingly change as well. These revengeful and vindictive perpetrators fear being exposed and their false public persona revealed to the masses they've fooled for years. Justice does not usually prevail for the targeted victims as the family court system is often part of the problem, but if you escape, you have a great chance of moving forward, starting over with rebuilding your life and finding peace, harmony and true love.

Abusers are also obsessed with stealing and manipulating money and are often fiscally irresponsible. Most victims find that their cash and assets have been suddenly depleted and their house goes into foreclosure even when for years they were told and believed that the family home was paid off. The victim learns that all of the joint charge cards are maxed out and new credit cards were fraudulently opened up with their forged name and social security number. These abusers engage in Identity Theft and even steal their own kids' money from their bank accounts, empty their college funds, cash in their savings bonds and take out credit cards in their children's names without them knowing, ruining their children's credit and future purchasing power. It's not until years later that you may find out that their urgent need for large sums of cash is to fund their double or triple life of pornography, gambling and/ or substance abuse addictions, private investments or even to support another family or children they never disclosed to you; many adult children are shocked to later find out that they have half siblings that were secretly kept from them.

DR. MARNI HILL FODERARO

A very common coping mechanism for the victims who are courageous enough to escape the abusive relationship is to try to make sense of how and why such bad things can happen to such good people. You play detective and begin to seek confirmation though your own investigations using computer searches, literature research, books, blogs, YouTube videos and podcasts and/or therapeutic counseling to get answers to your many questions in an attempt to put a name to your feelings and experiences. You quickly find that you are not alone and that there is a huge support network out there of professionals and everyday people who have experienced Domestic Violence, Narcissistic Abuse and/or Parental Alienation and often, as part of their own healing process, are driven to provide resources, support and awareness to others.

Recovering from the extreme complex trauma and stress of this type of abuse is a process and takes a great deal of time. It can be compared to other significant losses where you are forced to navigate through the stages of grief. You may have been able to move on or move far away to reclaim your life and start over, but you continue to be haunted by your experiences and dashed hopes for your future. Most of us have to deal with breaking trauma bonds and our abuser's continued emotional, physical, cyber or legal stalking and harassment for years. You may feel alone and lonely as your support system has vanished, although in time, this period of isolation proves to be helpful as you regain your independence and inner strength. During your recovery efforts of self-healing and self-love and to understand your role in this unfortunate situation, it is helpful to reflect and examine your family of origin dynamics and acknowledge your own childhood traumas, abandonment issues, core wounds and possible intergenerational abuse that most likely contributed to your naivety and unmet emotional needs which eventually led you to choosing toxic, controlling and abusive partnerships. This history may have contributed to you trusting too much too soon, being an over-giver or having weak boundaries, making you the perfect target for your abuser.

You probably came across this book as a result of your quest for information. Well, I'm glad you did and hopefully the timing was synchronistic. This book, *TRUE DECEIT FALSE LOVE: Survivor's Acrostic Poetry Workbook on Domestic Violence, Narcissistic Abuse & Parental Alienation* will hopefully provide you with much needed validation. Reading and creating acrostic poems will give you awareness to the plethora of words or statements associated with much of what you've experienced. This list of words is by no means complete, as new verbiage is being created daily. Check out the other volumes in the *TRUE DECEIT FALSE LOVE* series.

I take absolutely no credit in the development of any of these commonly-used terms and phrases as they have been coined by countless others and are regularly circulated amongst the abuse recovery community. Reading the terms & phrases in the poems (filled with information and emotion) and creating your own poems while you are simultaneously connecting the dots to your own experiences can be very therapeutic and an integral part of the healing process.

In closing, I would like to offer words of hope and encouragement to all of the men, women and children who find themselves navigating Domestic Violence, Narcissistic Abuse and/or Parental Alienation. Know that you are a beautiful, loving soul who should be treated with kindness and respect. You are not crazy. You didn't do anything to deserve the malicious treatment you received at the hands of your abuser and his/her Flying Monkeys. Don't be hard on yourself that it took you so long to finally see things for what they really are; abusers are skilled master-manipulators and put great efforts into hiding their venomous, vindictive and vile deceit behind their fraudulent mask. Remember, nobody is perfect and we are all here to learn life's lessons. You know the truth of what you've been through.

Try to look objectively at what's happened to you so you can unlearn negative patterns and steer away from unhealthy tendencies as you become more vigilant in recognizing abusive people and situations. The friends that you lose because you no longer resonate with them, their values or their behavior, make room for new relationships with like-minded people of integrity. Watch out for the Hoovers and Flying Monkeys. Be willing to change and get out of your comfort zone. Reflect on the values that are meaningful to you and stay true to them. Honor who you are. Acknowledge your feelings. Manage the triggers. Choose to respond, not react, to life's challenges. Embrace your authenticity as you gather up your strength to strive for independence and personal growth while you get back on your feet. You have what it takes to get through this. Knowledge is power.

Understanding ourselves, as well as learning the dynamics of toxic individuals who engage in Domestic Violence, Narcissistic Abuse and/ or Parental Alienation, can be very enlightening and help empower you to move towards peace and self-actualization. Your survivor voice matters. Turn your negative experiences into positive opportunities to evolve into the genuine person that you were meant to be. Don't be surprised if you experience some type of Spiritual Awakening and are now more in tune with the universe's signs and synchronicities. Have faith. This may be a good time to reconnect, embrace and trust in a Divine Higher Source. You never know, God could even come to your garage sale!

My sincere hope is that this acrostic poetry workbook *TRUE DECEIT FALSE LOVE: Survivor's Acrostic Poetry Workbook on Domestic Violence, Narcissistic Abuse & Parental Alienation* and the companion books of terms, phrases and poems will provide you with a creative outlet and much needed validation. Stay strong as you take back your power to live a beautiful and fulfilling life. You deserve more and the best is yet to come. Truth eventually prevails. I wish you compassion and goodness on your healing journey. Much love and light to you.

Many Blessings Always,

Marni

DR. MARNI HILL FODERARO

"A Mother's gift to her daughter sometimes comes before its time,
but its time will come as long as love and laughter light its way.

Will there be love and understanding, or will the lack
of acceptance and compassion continue on?"

~Elizabeth Ann Hill-Waldenmaier Hansen

(Born 9-29-1930 Transitioned 9-19-1996)

"Motherwords" letter to daughter Marni from her
Mama (1990) as she was "Passing The Pearls."

AUTHOR BIOGRAPHY

Marni Hill Foderaro is an award-winning and celebrated author, speaker and educator. She earned her doctorate in education and completed postdoctoral studies at Harvard after a very successful and rewarding 35-year career as a high school Special Education Teacher, with 12 years as a university Adjunct Professor. Marni is the esteemed author of *God Came to My Garage Sale*, a 2020 Best Books award-winning Spiritual fiction and *True Deceit False Love: 15,555 Terms & Phrases on Domestic Violence, Narcissistic Abuse & Parental Alienation*, both prominently endorsed. Marni is a lover of animals, nature, music and world travel and handles life's challenges with love and compassion. She values honesty, integrity, equality and goodness and prays for peace on earth. Marni was born in the South, raised her children in the Midwest and lives in the Caribbean. In addition to her speaking engagements and various writing endeavors on embracing Spirituality after surviving Domestic Violence, Narcissistic Abuse, Parental Alienation and Intergenerational Family Trauma, Marni is a contributing author to numerous anthology books, including: *The Last Breath, The Evolution of Echo, We're All In This Together: Embrace One Another, Passing The Pearls, The Ulti-MUTT Book for Dog Lovers* and volume 2 of *bLU Talks Presents: business, Life and the Universe.* Marni is the author of the 4-book series *TRUE DECEIT FALSE LOVE.* Dr. Marni Hill Foderaro's books, podcast interviews, guest articles and events can be found on her website.

www.GodCameToMyGarageSale.com

"When the heart is flooded with LOVE
there is no room in it for fear, for doubt, for hesitation."

~Anne Morrow Lindbergh
Author, Gift from the Sea

WHAT EXACTLY IS ACROSTIC POETRY AND HOW DO I CREATE IT?

Acrostic poetry refers to poems where the first letter of each line spells out a particular term or phrase. See examples in volumes 2 and 3 of the *TRUE DECEIT FALSE LOVE* book series.

Acrostic Poetry has been around for hundreds of years, from the Bible to Shakespeare, to current times. The word "acrostic" comes from the French "acrostiche" which originates from post-classical Latin "acrostichis." It also has Ancient Greek origins meaning "highest, topmost verse." Acrostics were common in Medieval literature in poetry, prose, verse and religious prayers. In modern times, many of us are familiar with organizational acronyms, where letters or initials are used to represent longer words, terms or phrases. If you want to get super-creative, you can challenge yourself to create acrostic poems that are more complex by writing Double Acrostics, using the same letters/initials at both the beginning and end of a line. Acrostic poems do not have to rhyme, have a specific meter or follow other poetry patterns. They can most definitely be free form and short or long, allowing you to creatively express your ideas or thoughts.

Along the same theme as Acrostic Poetry, there are some words that are "acronyms" which are formed from the initial components of longer terms or phrases and "backronyms" that are acronyms that are formed from an already existing term or phrase. One example is the AMBER ALERT program, named after Amber Hagerman, a 9-year-old girl who in 1996 was abducted and murdered. The backronym for AMBER is: "America's Missing: Broadcast Emergency Response." Another example is the APGAR score used to assess a newborn baby's health with APGAR standing for "Appearance, Pulse, Grimace, Activity and Respiration." An example that survivors of Family Violence may be familiar with is F.O.G. which stands for "Fear-Obligation-Guilt" or C.P.T.S.D. which stands for "Complex Post Traumatic Stress Disorder."

As a retired educator (after a very successful and rewarding 35-year career as a high school English/Resource/Special Education Teacher, with 12 years as a university adjunct professor) I often used acrostics as mnemonic devices or learning techniques to help students remember, retain and retrieve certain terms and phrases. One example was learning the planets in order: "My-Very-Earthy-Mother-Just-Sat-Upon-Nine-Pillows" stood for "Mercury-Venus-Earth-Mars-Jupiter-Saturn-Uranus-Neptune-and (the now no-longer) Pluto." I also used mnemonics to remember the keys/notes when reading music: FACE stands for the notes that fill the spaces in the treble clef, with the saying "Every Good Boy Deserves Fudge" for the notes EGBDF.

To survivors and others who want to use this *TRUE DECEIT FALSE LOVE* workbook and create their own Acrostic Poetry, just follow these simple steps:

1. **Choose a term or phrase from the suggested list or refer to the 15,555 Terms & Phrases from volume 1 of the series, or come up with your own personalized name or word.**

2. **Write that name, word, term or phrase vertically on the lined workbook page.**

3. **Think about what you want to say related to that chosen term or phrase.**

4. **Write a word or sentence that begins with each of the letters. You can make one or more longer sentences, making sure that each line starts with the next letter in your original vertical term or phrase.**

Now it's time for you to "put pen to paper" or use your computer's writing program to create your very own acrostic poetry. You can always refer to the terms, phrases and poems in *TRUE DECEIT FALSE LOVE* and follow the examples. Reading and creating these acrostic poems can be extremely therapeutic on your healing journey.

DR. MARNI HILL FODERARO

CONTENTS

A

<u>Suggested Terms & Phrases for your own acrostic poems:</u>
above the law, abuse, abuser, acceptance, accusations, addictions, adult
children, affair, affirmations, alienate, alienator, aligning with the
abuser, anger, antisocial, anxiety, apology, argument, arrogant, attack,
attorney, authenticity, authorities, autoimmune issues, awareness

Attachment-Based Model

A dvocate and clinical psychotherapist Dr. Craig A. Childress is an expert in

T he identification and treatment of one of

T he most devastating forms of Child

A buse: Parental Alienation. The innocent young or adult

C hild is used as a Weapon by his or

H er Narcissistic Personality-Disordered Parent

M ainly to reject and punish the Ex-Spouse for

E scaping the control and manipulation of their

N arcissistic Ex and that toxic relationship. Psychologically speaking,

T he complete suppression of the child's attachment and

B onding motivations toward the Loving, Normal-Range, Safe,

A vailable, Targeted Parent are severed and cut off completely. The

S plitting occurs once the child is conditioned to favor the

E motionally Abusive, Alienating Parent. Unfortunately, this need to

D estroy, "protect" and create a child-victim narrative with lies and implanted False

M emories results in Rejection and Estrangement that is difficult for the child and Loving Parent to

O vercome. Lives and families are ruined by this one Abuser. This Pathological

D estruction and Delusion is also directed at the Targeted Parent's entire

E xtended Family, so basically the child who Aligns with the Abusive Parent

L oses half of themselves. Parental Alienation is a Hate Crime.

Abandonment

A _____

B _____

A _____

N _____

D _____

O _____

N _____

M _____

E _____

N _____

T _____

DR. MARNI HILL FODERARO

AHA Moment

A _____

H _____

A _____

M _____

O _____

M _____

E _____

N _____

T _____

DR. MARNI HILL FODERARO

DR. MARNI HILL FODERARO

B

<u>Suggested Terms & Phrases for your own acrostic poems:</u>
backstabber, bait and hook, balancing act, bankruptcy, bashing,
battle, behavior, believe, belittling, best friend, betray, betrayal,
birthdays, black sheep, blame, blamed, blindsided, blocked, bonds,
borderline personality disorder, boss, brain fog, brainwashed, brave,
bravery, breadcrumbs, break the cycle, broke, broken, buying love

Bonds With Parents

B   onds between a child and their Loving Parent should not be broken;

O   nly with Parental Alienation do you see this happen. It's not

N   atural and indicates Attachment-Based Trauma.

D   ads and Moms should both be in their child's life. Stop breaking the bonds!

S   ons and daughters need both their dad and mom.

W   hen parents divorce it is

I   mportant for children

T   o know that they are loved.

H   owever, Abusive Alienators don't really care about their kids.

P   arents should not use their children as

A   mmunition or weapons as they seek

R   evenge on their Ex-Spouse who was able to

E   scape the Abuse and chaos.

N   o parent should be Alienated or Estranged from their children.

T   ake the high road and play nice. Stop trying to sever Family Bonds.

S   ick, vindictive Alienators are committing Child Abuse.

Boundaries

B _____

O _____

U _____

N _____

D _____

A _____

R _____

I _____

E _____

S _____

DR. MARNI HILL FODERARO

Broken Family

B _____

R _____

O _____

K _____

E _____

N _____

F _____

A _____

M _____

I _____

L _____

Y _____

DR. MARNI HILL FODERARO

DR. MARNI HILL FODERARO

C

<u>Suggested Terms & Phrases for your own acrostic poems:</u>
CPTSD, calculating, campaign of denigration, careful, carrying
on, cause and effect, change, character, charges, cheater, cheating,
child, child abuse, children, choices, closure, cluster B personality
disorder, codependent, coercive control, cognitive distortions,
cognitive empathy, college payments, compassion, competition,
competitive, complex trauma, con artist, confession, conflict,
confused, confusion, control, controlling, core wounds, counseling,
court corruption, court order, criminal, cross generational
coalition, cult leader, custody, cut ties, cycle of abuse

DR. MARNI HILL FODERARO

Covert Malignant Narcissists

C   harming, yet cunning, manipulative and secretive, unlike the

O   vert Narcissist, the Covert grooms each

V   ictim from day one. He very carefully selects an

E   mpath who is beautiful and intelligent with

R   esources he can plan to acquire after

T   he Love Bombing and Mirroring phases. In his need to Control, he

M   akes sure his Victim questions herself and relies on him for

A   nything and everything. At first it appears he

L   oves her and is looking out for her best interests, but

I   t doesn't take long for the Predator to

G   et a bit sloppy, revealing Red Flags to his Prey. The

N   arcissist is so slick, however, that the Empath

A   nd most everyone else, is fooled and

N   obody questions his inconsistencies, sneaky behavior or

T   he fact that despite living an extravagant life, there's

N   o money in the bank and he's constantly juggling funds and maxing out credit card

A   ccounts. He disappears unexpectedly. What he is doing is

R   euniting with old flames or scoping out fresh New Supply. He deceitfully

C   laims he's working late at the office and must travel extensively

I   n order to get ahead at his job. She believes him and

S   tarts taking care of everything home and family in addition to many jobs

S   o he can advance his career. She eventually gets run down and worn out.

I   n fact, her health begins to suffer. When

S   he asks him what's going on, he says she's paranoid, delusional and unappreciative. He eventually

T   rades her in for a newer model with no apologies to her or the kids.

S   tay away from Covert Malignant Narcissists.

Cognitive Dissonance

C _____

O _____

G _____

N _____

I _____

T _____

I _____

V _____

E _____

D _____

I _____

S _____

S _____

O _____

N _____

A _____

N _____

C _____

E _____

DR. MARNI HILL FODERARO

Crazymaking

C _____

R _____

A _____

Z _____

Y _____

M _____

A _____

K _____

I _____

N _____

G _____

DR. MARNI HILL FODERARO

DR. MARNI HILL FODERARO

D

<u>Suggested Terms & Phrases for your own acrostic poems:</u>
D.N.A., dad, daddy, damaged, dangerous, dark triad,
darkness, dating again, daughter, debt. deception, defeat,
defending yourself, defense mechanisms, deflection, delusional,
demoralize, denial, dependency, destitute, destructive, devalue
phase, devastated, disappointments, discarded, discounting,
dishonesty, disrespected, distorted reality, divorce, drama,
drama triangle, duping delight, dysfunctional relationship

Divide And Conquer

D   ivide and Conquer in Parental Alienation can be prevented

I   n High Conflict Divorce cases if the children are

V   alidated and there is no badmouthing and no

I   nconsistencies between mom's expectations and

D   ad's expectations. Children often fall Victim and

E   mploy this strategy themselves, thinking it's their idea.

A   s a result of Pathogenic Parenting, the Covert Malignant, Abusive,

N   arcissistic and Alienating Parent often uses the

D   ivide and Conquer technique as they refuse to and sabotage efforts to

C   o-Parent with their Ex-Spouse, the Loving, Normal-Range,

O   pposite Parent. These vindictive Child-Abusing

N   arcs use this tactic to systematically remove one parent from a child's life by

Q   uestioning their mental health and abilities, even though this was never an issue before the divorce.

U   nfair and unjust legal actions and rulings contribute to this un-

E   thical and devastating form of Child Abuse. Divide and Conquer, fear, dis-

R   espect and destroying families are unfortunately employed by the Favored Parent.

Dishonesty

D _____

I _____

S _____

H _____

O _____

N _____

E _____

S _____

T _____

Y _____

DR. MARNI HILL FODERARO

Domestic Violence

D _____

O _____

M _____

E _____

S _____

T _____

I _____

C _____

V _____

I _____

O _____

L _____

E _____

N _____

C _____

E _____

DR. MARNI HILL FODERARO

DR. MARNI HILL FODERARO

E

<u>Suggested Terms & Phrases for your own acrostic poems:</u>
egg shells, egocentric, emails, embolden lies, emergency,
emotions, empathy, empowered, empty threats, encouragement,
enemy, energy vampire, enmeshed, entitlement, equitable,
erased dad, erased family, erased mom, escape plan,
estrangement, evil, exploitation, expose the narcissist

Estranged Adult Children

E   stranged Adult Children

S   uffer so many Emotional Losses.

T   hey have been Coercively Controlled to

R   eject their Loving Normal-Range Parent

A   nd their entire side of that extended family.

N   ow these Adult Brainwashed Kids

G   o along living their lives believing

E   very lie and half-truth told to them.

D   ads and moms, please stop this Abuse to the

A   dult Children you are using to

D   estroy your Ex with. Don't you

U   nderstand that you alone are causing a

L   ifetime of damage and Trauma

T   o your own flesh and blood?

C   an these Adult Children recover from this

H   orrendous life sentence? Some do, only

I   f they learn about Parental Alienation and reclaim the

L   oving Parent-Child Bond of their Targeted

D   ad or Mom, who loves them so much. Please

R   eflect on the resulting consequences to you and your

E   ntire family. Your children deserve a happy life,

N   ot the Divide and Conquer life you are currently living in.

Emotional Abuse

E _____

M _____

O _____

T _____

I _____

O _____

N _____

A _____

L _____

A _____

B _____

U _____

S _____

E _____

DR. MARNI HILL FODERARO

Enmeshment

E _____

N _____

M _____

E _____

S _____

H _____

M _____

E _____

N _____

T _____

DR. MARNI HILL FODERARO

DR. MARNI HILL FODERARO

F

<u>Suggested Terms & Phrases for your own acrostic poems:</u>
failure, fairytale, faith, fake apology, false allegations,
false flattery, false security, false self, family, father, father
wound, fathers' rights, fear, feelings, fight or flight, financial
abuse, finding hope, fixed personality, flattery, flipping the
script, flirting, follow your dreams, forging documents,
forgiveness, forgotten memories, fraud, friends, friendship

Flying Monkeys

F   riends and family who previously

L   oved and supported you will be fooled by

Y   our Ex. Lies and half-truths will be

I   mparted to damage and destroy you

N   ow that you've Escaped the Toxic Relationship.

G   reat friends, neighbors, relatives and

M   any acquaintances, even co-workers, who

O   nce valued you, just stop talking with you.

N   ow they are loyal to and do the Bidding for your Ex. The Narc

K   nowingly uses these people to get any and

E   very little bit of information on

Y   ou. These Brainwashed people are now Flying Monkeys and

S   ecret field reporters for your Narcissistic Ex.

Final Discard

F _____

I _____

N _____

A _____

L _____

D _____

I _____

S _____

C _____

A _____

R _____

D _____

DR. MARNI HILL FODERARO

Final Straw

F _____

I _____

N _____

A _____

L _____

S _____

T _____

R _____

A _____

W _____

DR. MARNI HILL FODERARO

DR. MARNI HILL FODERARO

G

<u>Suggested Terms & Phrases for your own acrostic poems:</u>
gambling, games, generational abuse, generational domestic
violence, getting stronger, ghosted, goal post anxiety, goals,
God, going solo, golden child, goodbye, gossip, graduations
missed, grandiose, grandiose narcissist, grandiosity, grandparent
alienation, grey rock, grief, grieving, grieving parents,
grooming, guardian, guardian ad litem, guilty, gut feeling

DR. MARNI HILL FODERARO

Gaslighting

G	aslighting, a term from the 1944 movie, is the
A	ct of manipulating the Empath's understanding of
S	imple, everyday occurrences so the Victim
L	ooks crazy, as if they have a serious Mental Disorder. False
I	nformation is systematically said by the Narcissistic Abuser
G	etting the Empath Victim to question their sanity or
H	is or her memory or understanding of the
T	ruth. Narcs purposely engage Empaths
I	n this destructive tactic to keep their
N	arcissistic Supply dependent, isolated and questioning their reality.
G	etting disoriented and Gaslit by the Narc is a very common tactic.

Getting Stronger

G _____

E _____

T _____

T _____

I _____

N _____

G _____

S _____

T _____

R _____

O _____

N _____

G _____

E _____

R _____

DR. MARNI HILL FODERARO

Grateful

G _____

R _____

A _____

T _____

E _____

F _____

U _____

L _____

DR. MARNI HILL FODERARO

DR. MARNI HILL FODERARO

H

Suggested Terms & Phrases for your own acrostic poems:
half sibling, half-truths, hang in there, harassment, harem closet,
harem garage, harmful, hate, health, healthy boundaries, heart,
help me, hidden agenda, high conflict divorce, hindsight, holidays
missed, home, honor, honorable, hoover, hoovering, hope, hostile
aggressive parenting, hurt and rescue cycle, hypervigilance

Healing Journey

H	ealing from the Trauma of Family Violence is
E	ssential to be able to Recover from
A	busive Others. Freeing yourself is a start.
L	eaving your Abuser can be challenging.
I	n many cases the Domestic Violence does
N	ot end after you Escape. The Abuser
G	aslit you to question your abilities and worth. The
J	ourney involves reclaiming your Peace
O	r more importantly, your Safety. You may experience
U	ncomfortable feelings of guilt, depression, sadness,
R	age, anxiety and stress. In time you will
N	ot be as Triggered and you can get back to
E	njoying life and fulfilling
Y	our purpose and passion. It's a journey to heal.

Half Truths

H _____

A _____

L _____

F _____

T _____

R _____

U _____

T _____

H _____

S _____

DR. MARNI HILL FODERARO

Heartbroken

H   _____

E   _____

A   _____

R   _____

T   _____

B   _____

R   _____

O   _____

K   _____

E   _____

N   _____

DR. MARNI HILL FODERARO

DR. MARNI HILL FODERARO

Suggested Terms & Phrases for your own acrostic poems:
I love you, idealization phase, identity theft, ignore the red flags,
ignored, illegal, image, image envy, implant false memories, in laws,
incest, incest abuse, induced trauma, ineffective counsel, inflated ego,
injustice, inner circle, inner peace, innocent, intelligence, intermittent
reinforcement, intimidation, intuition, invalidation, isolation

Independent Thinker Phenomenon

I   ndependent Thinker Phenomenon in

N   ow Alienated Adult Children whose relationship with one parent is

D   estroyed, refers to the claim that

E   ven though there were never, ever any

P   roblems before the divorce and the parent and child previously

E   njoyed a loving, healthy relationship their entire lives,

N   ow after the divorce the child immediately Rejects either the

D   ad or mom because they believe

E   very lie or half-truth told to them by one of them and

N   ow want nothing to do with

T   heir other Loving, now-Targeted Parent.

T   hese Adult Kids currently claim that their "Bad" Parent

H   ad to have done something so very wrong

I   n their parenting that they can

N   o longer have anything to do with them.

K   ids will unknowingly

E   xperience Stockholm Syndrome where they

R   eject the Loving Parent and Align with the Abusing, Alienating

P   arent. People in general tend to believe these Adult Kids,

H   onoring and wrongly agreeing that these Targeted Parents must have

E   ngaged in Abusing their child or the child would

N   ot cut them out of their lives.

O   nly, that logic couldn't be farther from the Truth. Alienating

M   others or Fathers can systematically

E   nmesh their Adult Children into going

N   o-Contact with their other Loving Parent, or even their siblings. This is

O   ne of the many tactics Abusers use to

N   egate the natural loving Family Bonds and punish their Ex for leaving.

Infidelity

I _____

N _____

F _____

I _____

D _____

E _____

L _____

I _____

T _____

Y _____

DR. MARNI HILL FODERARO

Intimate Partner Abuse

I _____

N _____

T _____

I _____

M _____

A _____

T _____

E _____

P _____

A _____

R _____

T _____

N _____

E _____

R _____

A _____

B _____

U _____

S _____

E _____

DR. MARNI HILL FODERARO

DR. MARNI HILL FODERARO

J

Suggested Terms & Phrases for your own acrostic poems:
jackknifed fairytale, jail, jekyll and hyde, jezebel, jinxed, joint custody, journaling, judges, judicial corruption, judgment, juggling act, juggling supply, jump effect, just a phase, justice, justice denied, justified estrangement, justified rage

DR. MARNI HILL FODERARO

Jigsaw Puzzle

J   ust like the effort it takes to assemble

I   nterlocking and mosaic pieces to

G   et the big picture—navigating

S   evere Domestic Violence is like doing

A   jigsaw puzzle. More and more Truths slowly come out

W   hen you Escape your Abuser and you are trying to

P   ut the puzzle pieces together and

U   nderstand what happened in your relationship. Abusers have

Z   ero guilt for how the treated you because they have

Z   ero Empathy. Targets often innocently and willingly

L   et Abusers into their lives without knowing you were chosen and that

E   verything was a set up. It takes years to put the pieces of the puzzle together.

Jealousy

J _____

E _____

A _____

L _____

O _____

U _____

S _____

Y _____

Journey

J   _____

O   _____

U   _____

R   _____

N   _____

E   _____

Y   _____

DR. MARNI HILL FODERARO

DR. MARNI HILL FODERARO

K

<u>Suggested Terms & Phrases for your own acrostic poems:</u>
karpman drama triangle, keep the faith, keep up your radar, keeping secrets, keeping up with the Joneses, kernel of truth, kicked to the curb, kidnapped children, kidnapped minds, kids, kin, kind, kindness, kiss, kiss of death, knight in shining armor, knocked down, knocked up, know your enemy, knowing the truth, knowledge is power, kryptonite

Kids Need Both Parents

K   ids need to have both parents

I   n their lives. When I chose to

D   ivorce our children's father in December, I made

S   ure that he was invited and welcomed for Christmas. I would

N   ever Alienate our kids from their dad,

E   ven after realizing how Deceitful and Abusive he was.

E   very child needs both of their parents. I believe that

D   ads and moms should both be in their kids' lives.

B   ut the Narcissistic Abusers have

O   ther plans when it comes to

T   heir actions and reactions. Their father was

H   ell-bent on a mission to Destroy me as a

P   erson when I did not obey his threats

A   bout what would happen if I divorced him. His True Character was

R   evealed. He acted like he was

E   ager to work together for the kids, but in reality he was

N   ot. He set out to Alienate our children from me,

T   hen he even Alienated and Isolated the

S   iblings from each other. Ideally kids should have both parents in their lives.

Karma

K   _____

A   _____

R   _____

M   _____

A   _____

DR. MARNI HILL FODERARO

Keeping Secrets

K _____

E _____

E _____

P _____

I _____

N _____

G _____

S _____

E _____

C _____

R _____

E _____

T _____

S _____

DR. MARNI HILL FODERARO

DR. MARNI HILL FODERARO

L

<u>Suggested Terms & Phrases for your own acrostic poems:</u>
lack of empathy, learned helplessness, leaving your abuser, legal
abuse, lessons learned, letting go, liar, lie under oath, life, life
choices, light vs. dark, listen to your gut intuition, living dead,
living hell, living will, loneliness, lonely, losing custody, losing
your children, loss, losses, lost child, lost hope, love, love child,
love triangle, low contact, low self-esteem, loyalty, lying

Losing Friends and Neighbors

L ots of people don't understand Family Abuse

O r they refuse to help Victims because they

S ay they are neutral and don't want to get

I nvolved. Well, these people are actually supporting the

N arcissistic Abuser. He or she will

G et friends and neighbors and even

F amily members against the Target, so any

R elationship support is not there for the Victim.

I n effect, the tactics that Abusers

E ngage in involves a major and Covert Smear Campaign.

N ow when you need support the most, you

D on't have it. Your character, credibility and

S o often your reputation has been undermined.

A person that previously enjoyed a

N umber of friendships, now has these relationships so

D amaged, just because the Malevolent

N arcissistic Abuser wants

E veryone to Abandon you.

I t's all based on outright lies and half-truths.

G etting your Support System against you and

H aving you left Isolated and Traumatized

B y losing friends and family is just

O ne of the many ways Abusers Abuse. They

R eally want you Punished for leaving them

S o that they can appear as the Victim.

Living In Fear

L _____

I _____

V _____

I _____

N _____

G _____

I _____

N _____

F _____

E _____

A _____

R _____

DR. MARNI HILL FODERARO

Love Bombing

L _____

O _____

V _____

E _____

B _____

O _____

M _____

B _____

I _____

N _____

G _____

DR. MARNI HILL FODERARO

DR. MARNI HILL FODERARO

M

<u>Suggested Terms & Phrases for your own acrostic poems:</u>
malevolent, malicious, malignant narcissist, manifesting,
manufactured lies, marriage, marry me, mascot, mask, mask slipped,
master manipulator, maternal alienation, mean, mean spirited,
mediation, mental abuse, mental home, milestones, mind control,
mindful, mini-me, minimizing, miracles, mirroring, misfortune,
missed milestones, missing your kids, mistakes, mistrust, mom,
mommy, money, monkey branching, moods, moody, morality, morals,
mother, mother wound, mourning, moving the goal posts, murder

Marginalization

M   arginalization is when you

A   re minimized by the Deceitful and

R   uthless Covert Narcissist. They will

G   aslight you to make you feel extremely

I   nsignificant. They want you to believe that you are

N   ot worthy or should be valued in

A   ny way. These Abusers act like they

L   ove you, yet their calculated actions

I   nvalidate you. You eventually lose your

Z   est for life and become Isolated. They

A   lienate you from your friends and family so

T   hat you lose the relationships you previously had or currently have

I   n your life. Nothing you think, say or do matters. You are Marginalized.

O   thers start to put you down too, even your own children, who are taught to hate!

N   arcissists win at this game until you recognize the Abuse and Escape.

Manipulation

M _____

A _____

N _____

I _____

P _____

U _____

L _____

A _____

T _____

I _____

O _____

N _____

DR. MARNI HILL FODERARO

Memories

M   _____

E   _____

M   _____

O   _____

R   _____

I   _____

E   _____

S   _____

DR. MARNI HILL FODERARO

DR. MARNI HILL FODERARO

N

<u>Suggested Terms & Phrases for your own acrostic poems:</u>
naive alienator, narcissist, narcissistic abuse, narcissistic fluffing,
narcissistic injury, narcissistic rage, narcissistic smirk and stare,
narcopath, narrow-minded, natural bonds, need for power,
needy, neglect, neglected, negotiations, neighbors, nest egg,
neutrality, new start, new supply, nightmare, no boundaries,
no contact, no remorse, nowhere to hide, numbing the pain

DR. MARNI HILL FODERARO

Narcissistic Supply

N   arcissistic Supply involves a constant need for

A   doration, adulation and admiration as he tries to

R   egulate his labile and ego-driven Self-

C   oncept, sense of superiority and

I   mportance. Perception is

S   tronger than the Truth or Reality.

S   upply boosts the Narc's Grandiose Ego and

I   n his validation efforts to gain attention and gratification from his

S   upply, who he undermines and Grooms to be Submissive,

T   hese Narcs boast about any past accomplishments. He

I   dealizes his Target at first and then breaks down and Destroys. This

C   on-Man lives for the reaction of the

S   ource to his Triggers to get his Narcissistic Supply with

U   ndeserving attention. The Narc's Supply is a

P   erson who is being trained and Exploited. The Target is

P   erishable. The Narcissist consumes her and others after

L   ove-Bombing, then there is a need to recycle and replenish.

Y   ou are just being used. It's all a juggling act.

Negative Influences

N _____

E _____

G _____

A _____

T _____

I _____

V _____

E _____

I _____

N _____

F _____

L _____

U _____

E _____

N _____

C _____

E _____

S _____

DR. MARNI HILL FODERARO

No Contact

N   _____

O   _____

C   _____

O   _____

N   _____

T   _____

A   _____

C   _____

T   _____

DR. MARNI HILL FODERARO

DR. MARNI HILL FODERARO

O

<u>Suggested Terms & Phrases for your own acrostic poems:</u>
obedience, obligations, obsession, obsessive alienator, obstacles,
offended, omnipotent, on the rebound, one step ahead, open
wounds, open your eyes, opportunities, oppositional, out of control,
out of time, outlandish lies, outside influences, outsmart the
narcissist, overcoming adversity, overinflated ego, overt narcissist

Outsmarting The Narcissist

O utsmarting the Narcissist involves

U nderstanding that these Abusers

T wist the narratives to exonerate themselves and

S mear their Targets to cause them great Harm.

M anipulation and covert tactics

A re used to discredit good people.

R ealizing that not everyone has

T he Core Values of honesty, goodness and

I ntegrity can help a Target understand that

N arcissists have an Evil Agenda and

G o to great lengths to put down others as

T hey hide behind a False Mask of Deceit.

H ow do you outsmart these Abusers?

E ven though it may feel good, do

N ot get involved and play their game.

A great strategy is to carefully respond (or not) as opposed to

R eacting to their antics. They love to engage in Conflict, so going No-

C ontact can preserve your Dignity and Peace, even your safety.

I believe the best revenge is really not revenge at all:

S imply remove yourself from any interactions with your Abuser and

S pend your efforts focused on yourself.

I nvest in your own happiness and live a

S tress-free and happy life. Narcissists love

T he chaos and control and you don't need to feed into that.

Overcoming Obstacles

O   _____

V   _____

E   _____

R   _____

C   _____

O   _____

M   _____

I   _____

N   _____

G   _____

O   _____

B   _____

S   _____

T   _____

A   _____

C   _____

L   _____

E   _____

S   _____

DR. MARNI HILL FODERARO

Own Your Truth

O   _____

W   _____

N   _____

Y   _____

O   _____

U   _____

R   _____

T   _____

R   _____

U   _____

T   _____

H   _____

DR. MARNI HILL FODERARO

DR. MARNI HILL FODERARO

P

<u>Suggested Terms & Phrases for your own acrostic poems:</u>
pain, parallel parenting, paralyzed, parasympathetic nervous system, parent, parent alienation, parent-child bond, parent's rights, partner, partner abuse, passive aggressive, paternal alienation, paternity test, pathogenic parenting, pathological liar, pathological narcissism, patience, pattern, patterns of abuse, peace, people pleaser, perceived superiority, perceptions, perfect family, perfect partner, perfectionism, personality disorder, pink cloud syndrome, pity party, player, playing games, pornography, predator vs. prey, priorities, privacy, projection, psychological abuse, psychopath, psychopathy, punishment, put downs

DR. MARNI HILL FODERARO

Parental Alienation Awareness Day

P   arental Alienation Awareness Day

A   pril 25th

R   ecognized in 2006 by a Georgia governor

E   strangement is heart wrenching

N   ational Coalition Against Parental Alienation

T   eaching children to hate the other parent is wrong

A   ctivism and Awareness is key. Great advocate for "keeping families together" is AGAPE

L   OVE DOMINATES nonprofit with Parental Alienation survivor and advocate Tamara Gerstemeier Sweeney

A   lienators use children as Weapons against their Ex

L   ove one another. Let children love both parents.

I   nternational Support Network of Alienated Families-ISNAF

E   nmeshed with the Abuser, kids choose the Abuser's side and Align with the Alienator

N   evada governor recognized this in 2007

A   lways involves psychological manipulation and control

T   he Center for Judicial Excellence argues against PA

I   nstitute on Violence, Abuse, and Trauma-IVAT opposes

O   ur children will have lifelong relationship issues

N   arcissists must control with Power and Deceit

A   merican Professional Society on Abuse of Children-APSAC doesn't support PA

W   inning and competition by Covert Narcissists, undiagnosed of course

A   ll children deserve love from both parents

R   ichard A. Gardner introduced the term PAS

E   vents were formed, like "Bubbles of Love" or "Message in a Bottle"

N   onprofits were started worldwide

E   ventually Alienated Children may be intergenerationally Alienated by their own children

S   arvy Emily was a pioneer

S   ons and daughters are Traumatized

D   omestic Violence includes this Child Abuse

A   lienation has devastating and lifelong effects

Y   our voices matter: acknowledge Parental Alienation Awareness Day.

Panic Attack

P _____

A _____

N _____

I _____

C _____

A _____

T _____

T _____

A _____

C _____

K _____

DR. MARNI HILL FODERARO

Psychological Abuse

P _____

S _____

Y _____

C _____

H _____

O _____

L _____

O _____

G _____

I _____

C _____

A _____

L _____

A _____

B _____

U _____

S _____

E _____

DR. MARNI HILL FODERARO

DR. MARNI HILL FODERARO

Q

Suggested Terms & Phrases for your own acrostic poems:
Q.D.R.O., quality supply, quantum healing, quashed
dreams, queen, quest, questioning yourself, questions
unanswered, quick thinking, quid pro quo, quiet panic
attack, quiet rage, quintessential, quitting, quizzed

Qualified Experts

Q   ualified by their degrees, education and positions,

U   ltimately these experts play

A   large role in the outcomes of whether the

L   oving, Normal-Range Parent

I   s deemed unfit and unable to properly care

F   or their children, even though their parenting was wonderful before the divorce.

I   nvolved in making recommendations, court

E   xperts, with very limited knowledge, influence Custody and

D   o not know or care about the complete devastation they are doing to families. There are

E   xtreme consequences of their involvement as experts on Children's Welfare.

X   -Husbands and X-Wives get further Abused by

P   rofessionals who serve as Qualified

E   xperts because these experts are

R   eally financially connected to the courts and

T   he judges, so they are not impartial.

S   uch harm can be done by these so called "Qualified Experts."

Quest For The Truth

Q _____

U _____

E _____

S _____

T _____

F _____

O _____

R _____

T _____

H _____

E _____

T _____

R _____

U _____

T _____

H _____

DR. MARNI HILL FODERARO

Questions

Q

U

E

S

T

I

O

N

S

_____

_____

_____

_____

_____

_____

_____

_____

DR. MARNI HILL FODERARO

DR. MARNI HILL FODERARO

R

<u>Suggested Terms & Phrases for your own acrostic poems:</u>
rage, raped, ratio, reacting, reactions, reactive abuse, reality check,
rebellious, rebound, rebuilding my life, reclaim my life, reconciliation,
reconnect with my kids, reconnection, recover, recovered children,
recovered memories, recruiting new supply, red flags, red flags ignored,
red tape, reflex, refuel, refuge, regain control, regrets, reinvent yourself,
rejected parent, relationships, relatives, remarriage, remorse, repeated
abuse, rescued, resentful, resilience, respond don't react, respondent,
response, responsibilities, resources, reunification therapy, reward and
punishment, rewards, rewriting history, rewritten memories, risks,
risky behavior, rock bottom, role model, roles, romance, romantic

DR. MARNI HILL FODERARO

Reinventing Yourself

R   einventing yourself after surviving Abuse.

E   ventually you reach a point where a major change

I   n your life is warranted. You're a Survivor.

N   ow is the time to re-

V   isit your interests and passions. It's

E   ssential to evaluate your Core Values.

N   obody really knows you like you do.

T   ry not to let others tell you or

I   nstruct you on how you are to be or

N   ot to be. Reinvention involves

G   oing forward into new and unchartered territory.

Y   ou must acknowledge your strengths and/

O   r challenges and make a plan to

U   nderstand the steps you need to

R   ealize your dreams.

S   urvivors of Narcissistic Abuse are

E   ncouraged to reinvent themselves, but not a

L   ot is out there on how to Recover and move on.

F   ind your passions and follow your dreams.

Red Flags

R   _____

E   _____

D   _____

F   _____

L   _____

A   _____

G   _____

S   _____

DR. MARNI HILL FODERARO

Rejection

R _____

E _____

J _____

E _____

C _____

T _____

I _____

O _____

N _____

DR. MARNI HILL FODERARO

DR. MARNI HILL FODERARO

S

<u>Suggested Terms & Phrases for your own acrostic poems:</u>
sabotaged, sacrifice, sad, sadist, sadistic, safety, sandbagging,
sanity, saving grace, scammed, scapegoat child, scars, scheming,
script, scruples, second chances, secret agent, secrets, security,
seduction, self-absorbed, self care, self confidence, selfish,
separation, set up, sever parent-child bonds, sex, sexual abuse,
sexual harassment, sexually assaulted, shame, shattered dreams,
shock, siblings, silence, silent treatment, smear campaign, smirk,
snapped, social media, sorrow, spiritual bypassing, spousal abuse,
spouse, spreading lies, stalking, stare, status, stolen assets, stolen
children, stonewalling, strength, suicidal, superior, superiority

Stockholm Syndrome

S   tockholm, Sweden's 1973 six-day bank robbery created

T   rauma Bonding with the Victims

O   f Abuse where they identified with and were sympathetic to their

C   aptors' agenda and demands. The Sveriges

K   reditbanken's employees were held in a vault. These four

H   ostages developed a Pathological Alliance

O   r connection during and after this standoff.

L   ike the famous case where newspaper Heiress Patty Hearst

M   ost likely found Sympathy with her captors, her

S   urvival Strategy was to rob a California bank with them.

Y   ou, as a Adult Child Victim of one of your parent's Covert Malignant

N   arcissistic Abuse, may experience the Stockholm Syndrome in your

D   omestic Violence situation where you Estrange from the Loving, Safe Parent,

R   efusing to accept the reality

O   f the terrible treatment given to you by your Abuser. Young

M   en and women can both be Victims and Perpetrators.

E   motions and Trauma influence this extreme survival instinct.

Self Love

S _____

E _____

L _____

F _____

L _____

O _____

V _____

E _____

DR. MARNI HILL FODERARO

Survivor

S _____

U _____

R _____

V _____

I _____

V _____

O _____

R _____

DR. MARNI HILL FODERARO

DR. MARNI HILL FODERARO

T

<u>Suggested Terms & Phrases for your own acrostic poems:</u>
take control, taking sides, taking the bait, target, targeted
parent, taught to hate, tears, temper, tension, terrified,
thankful, therapist, therapy, thoughts, threatening, threats,
thriver, thrown away, time, tired, togetherness, too good to be
true, tormented, tough love, toxic, toxicity, tracking devices,
traditions, trafficked, tragedy, transference, transformation,
transgenerational alienation, trap, trapped, trash, trash talking,
trauma, trauma bonds, triangulation, trust, truth, truth telling

DR. MARNI HILL FODERARO

Temporary Restraining Order

T   rembling, I drove to my local police station with the

E   xpectation I could receive protection from my Covert

M   alignant Narcissist Abusing Ex-Husband. The

P   olice Officer was very kind as he

O   bjectively took my statement. He

R   eferred me to the police social worker who

A   ttentively listened, saying that unfortunately a

R   eally large number of Ex-Wives experience

Y   ears of Harassment and Stalking, especially if they

R   ightfully chose to leave their Abuser and filed for a PFA.

E   ventually I received counseling from the

S   ystem's Domestic Violence Unit to get a

T   emporary Restraining Order.

R   enewing it would be the only way my

A   buser would be ordered to leave me alone.

I   n that month of the Temporary Restraining Order, I did

N   ot hear or see my Ex and for once the Stalking stopped.

I   felt relieved and safe. That was short-lived. An advocate stood

N   ext to me in court. It's a terrible legal practice that when you

G   o to court for a Permanent Order, you have to face your Perpetrator. I

O   bserved the judge winking at my Ex's lawyer as his

R   esponse was given, of course filled with lies and their specific

D   ates on their professional-looking spreadsheet.

E   ven though I had video evidence of the Stalking, the judge

R   efused to look at it and my PFA request was dropped, just like that.

Trauma Bonding

T _____

R _____

A _____

U _____

M _____

A _____

B _____

O _____

N _____

D _____

I _____

N _____

G _____

DR. MARNI HILL FODERARO

Triggers

T   _____

R   _____

I   _____

G   _____

G   _____

E   _____

R   _____

S   _____

DR. MARNI HILL FODERARO

DR. MARNI HILL FODERARO

U

<u>Suggested Terms & Phrases for your own acrostic poems:</u>
unacceptable, unbelievable, uncomfortable, unconditional love,
uncooperative, uncover the truth, under the radar, underestimated
target, undermined, understanding suicide, understanding what
happened, undiagnosed narcissist, unending grief, unethical,
unfaithful, unfit parent, unfounded allegations, unfriending,
unhappy, unhealed wounds, unloved, unmasked, unresolved anger,
unsafe, unsent letters and gifts, unstable, upstanding, upstanding
public image, used and abused, using children as weapons, using fear

Unmask The Covert Narcissist

U   nmasking the Covert Malignant

N   arcissist may result in a

M   assive Collapse and Injury. These Abusers

A   re used to Controlling and Manipulating others in

S   ecret Agent form. Victims don't always

K   now the Evil that they are dealing with until

T   he Abusers accidentally confess to their wrongdoings or

H   ave some truth of their lies

E   xposed. They thrive on a False Narrative and

C   on others, pretending to be someone

O   ther than who they really are.

V   ery often they hurt those who are honest,

E   mpathetic, loving, generous, trusting and caring.

R   ealizing the True Character of

T   hese Abusers is devastating.

N   arcissists are Predators and don't let

A   ny of their Prey go quietly. The Harassment continues for years. You

R   eally should create an Exit Strategy where you

C   an avoid an obvious confrontation.

I   t is in your best interest to focus on your

S   afety as you get your affairs in order, especially your finances.

S   o many Victims leave

I   mmediately and then find themselves

S   tripped of all safety, support, money and even their innocent children.

T   ry to protect yourself when you Unmask the Covert Narcissist.

Unappreciated

U _____

N _____

A _____

P _____

P _____

R _____

E _____

C _____

I _____

A _____

T _____

E _____

D _____

DR. MARNI HILL FODERARO

Unravel The Truth

U   _____

N   _____

R   _____

A   _____

V   _____

E   _____

L   _____

T   _____

H   _____

E   _____

T   _____

R   _____

U   _____

T   _____

H   _____

DR. MARNI HILL FODERARO

DR. MARNI HILL FODERARO

V

<u>Suggested Terms & Phrases for your own acrostic poems:</u>
V.I.P., validation, values, vendetta, venomous, vicious cycle, victim, victim blaming, victim card, victim shaming, video binging, vigilance, vigilant, vindictive, vindictive crazy ex, violated, violating court orders, violations, violence, virtue signaling, virtues, visitation, voice, void of empathy, volatile, vows, vulnerable narcissist

DR. MARNI HILL FODERARO

Violating Court Orders

V   iolation of Court Orders happens often

I   n divorce cases where

O   ne party believes they are above the

L   aw and that Society's Rules don't

A   pply to them. Committing Contempt of

T   he Court Orders is serious and should really

I   nvolve civil and/or criminal penalties, but

N   arcissists somehow seem to evade

G   etting any fines or

C   onsequences when they don't follow Court

O   rders. This makes the Innocent Victims feel that the courts are

U   njust and Corrupt. It's disheartening to

R   ealize that justice does not usually prevail in

T   hese cases. Lawyers want you to enforce

O   rders by filing motions of contempt, but

R   eally what many want with contentious

D   ivorce cases is to rack up huge legal fees, so they

E   ncourage you to keep

R   e-engaging in this Legal Harassment. It's a costly, vicious

S   cenario with little accountability for the Abusers who don't follow Court Orders.

Validation

V _____

A _____

L _____

I _____

D _____

A _____

T _____

I _____

O _____

N _____

Verbal Abuse

V _____

E _____

R _____

B _____

A _____

L _____

A _____

B _____

U _____

S _____

E _____

DR. MARNI HILL FODERARO

DR. MARNI HILL FODERARO

W

<u>Suggested Terms & Phrases for your own acrostic poems:</u>
walking on eggshells, wake up call, warnings, warrior, watershed
moment, wayward black sheep, weak, weakness, wealth, weaponized
children, weapons, wedding, welfare, welfare of children, well-being,
white picket fence, why, why me, will to survive, winning, wisdom,
withholding, withholding affection, witness, woke, womanizer,
word salad, worthless, wounded children, wrongly arrested

Wolves In Sheep's Clothing

W   ho deceives? A Malignant Covert Narcissist does.

O   ur belief is that people are basically good and don't

L   ie, but that is not always our reality. We easily become

V   ictims. Years and years go by where we think

E   verything in our marriage is fine. The False Mask

S   lips and we come to learn that there are Dysfunctions:

I   nfidelities, financial manipulations, Smearing and Gaslighting. We

N   ever in a million years thought we married a

S   ecret Agent Man or Woman. What a complete

H   oax. We were defrauded and cheated out of our "Happily

E   ver After." These Narcs fooled us and used the kids as weapons. They

E   xploit and engage in the unthinkable Child Abuse Tactic of

P   arental Alienation as they Brainwash and

S   teal your children from you, the good, Loving and Targeted Parent.

C   hildren should never be taught to hate one parent and

L   ove the other parent. Children need BOTH

O   f their parents to feel Loved and

T   o feel Validated. You perseverate and keep asking yourself:

H   ow can this happen to our family? Who really

I   s this person I married and lived with for decades? A Wolf in Sheep's Clothing.

N   ow you've lost everything: the house, your assets, your money, your friends, the neighbors, the

G   arden, your health, your job and worse, the loving relationship with your kids.

Walking Away

W _____

A _____

L _____

K _____

I _____

N _____

G _____

A _____

W _____

A _____

Y _____

Web Of Lies

W _____

E _____

B _____

O _____

F _____

L _____

I _____

E _____

S _____

DR. MARNI HILL FODERARO

DR. MARNI HILL FODERARO

X

Suggested Terms & Phrases for your own acrostic poems:
x called the cops, x changing the kids, x erased, x husband, x
partner, x rated pornography, x spouse, x wife, xanadu, xanax, xenial
shame, xenology, xenoparasite, xeroxing documents, xmas ruined

X-Rated Pornography

X -rated Teen Pornography was found by the police

R ight on our family's computer

A fter my Ex-Husband moved out. He covertly went

T o great extremes to delete and

E rase his inappropriate searches, but forgot one. Narcissists aren't loyal and

D on't honor their vows. They have numerous affairs and watch

P orn to satisfy their insatiable need for power, attention

O r control. They are often sex-addicted. Narcs are

R eally threatened by a partner's basic sexual or emotional

N eeds and are incapable of feeling or

O penly expressing Love through intimacy.

G ratification is gained by watching pornography because it

R equires no empathy, no connection and no reciprocity.

A great many themes of Degradation, Control and

P ower are easily accessed online. Narcs are incapable of

H aving a healthy sex life with their spouse as they are always

Y earning to Mask their major intimacy deficits.

X-Hoovering

X   _____

H   _____

O   _____

O   _____

V   _____

E   _____

R   _____

I   _____

N   _____

G   _____

DR. MARNI HILL FODERARO

X-Spouse Erased

X _____

S _____

P _____

O _____

U _____

S _____

E _____

E _____

R _____

A _____

S _____

E _____

D _____

DR. MARNI HILL FODERARO

DR. MARNI HILL FODERARO

<u>Suggested Terms & Phrases for your own acrostic poems:</u>
Yahawhah, yanked by proxy abuse, yearning for justice, yelling, yellow rock, yen for safety, yo-yo effect, yobbish psychopaths, you are too sensitive, you misunderstood, you owe me, your happy place, your heart is broken, your honor, your self-love, you're a monster, you're too sensitive, YouTube video support

Your Kids Will Come Back

Y   our kids will return is a common response from

O   utsiders who mean well, but don't really

U   nderstand. Parental Alienation is difficult to

R   ecognize, even for professionals. To be Rejected by your

K   ids and watching them slip away from you

I   s like witnessing the Emotional

D   eath of Living Children. Your Alienating Ex-

S   pouse is severing your Loving Relationship

W   ith the kids and gets them to Align with Evil.

I   f children are to survive this Abusive, Polarized

L   ife, they have to distort reality, subconsciously engage in Splitting, which

L   ends itself to Independent Thinker Phenomenon. These children now

C   laim that their Loving, Normal-Range Parent is Dangerous

O   r Abusive, when this narrative is Falsely Implanted into their hearts and minds by the

M   alevolent Alienating Parent. Our children are in

E   ffect being Brainwashed in cult-like fashion.

B   eing aware and educating yourself on Parental

A   lienation helps Targeted Parents make sense of what's happened

C   ognitively, but this knowledge won't miraculously bring your

K   ids back to you. I pray for my children's Lightbulb Moment and that they come back.

Yearning For Justice

Y _____

E _____

A _____

R _____

N _____

I _____

N _____

G _____

F _____

O _____

R _____

J _____

U _____

S _____

T _____

I _____

C _____

E _____

DR. MARNI HILL FODERARO

You Are Not Crazy

Y   _____

O   _____

U   _____

A   _____

R   _____

E   _____

N   _____

O   _____

T   _____

C   _____

R   _____

A   _____

Z   _____

Y   _____

DR. MARNI HILL FODERARO

DR. MARNI HILL FODERARO

Z

<u>Suggested Terms & Phrases for your own acrostic poems:</u>
zany, zapped energy, zealous inducer, zenith awakening, zero
trust, zest for power, zilch contact, zinger deflections, zipped-
lipped slander, zombie, zombie control, zoned out, zugzwanged

Zigzagging The Truth

Z   igzaggers are liars. You can see them

I   n your work place. They can

G   ain your Trust in the office and then

Z   ap you behind your back to discredit you. There

A   re many lying Zigzaggers who employ Deception as they

G   auge who they can take advantage of.

G   etting to know the types of liars in the workplace

I   s helpful so you can

N   avigate how you deal with them.

G   enerally, the three types of liars are: First

T   he Pathetic Liar who is the colleague that wants to

H   ave you as their friend, avoiding conflicts with

E   xaggerated reasons why they don't do their share. Secondly,

T   here is the Narcissistic Liar who denies workplace

R   esponsibility, blames others and demands respect.

U   tmost damage can be done by the third type,

T   he Sociopath Liar, because they Zigzag and

H   ave no conscience and are habitually dishonest.

Zero Contact

Z   _____

E   _____

R   _____

O   _____

C   _____

O   _____

N   _____

T   _____

A   _____

C   _____

T   _____

DR. MARNI HILL FODERARO

Zest For Life

Z _____

E _____

S _____

T _____

F _____

O _____

R _____

L _____

I _____

F _____

E _____

DR. MARNI HILL FODERARO

DR. MARNI HILL FODERARO

My sincere hope is that this acrostic poetry workbook *TRUE DECEIT FALSE LOVE: Survivor's Acrostic Poetry Workbook on Domestic Violence, Narcissistic Abuse & Parental Alienation* and the companion books of terms, phrases and poems will provide you with a creative outlet and much needed validation.

Stay strong as you take back your power
to live a beautiful and fulfilling life.

You deserve more and the best is yet to come.

Truth eventually prevails.

I wish you compassion and goodness
on your healing journey.

Marni

Printed in the United States
by Baker & Taylor Publisher Services